Kilmann-Covin Organizational Influence Survey

RALPH H. KILMANN
TERESA JOYCE COVIN

Distributed by
KILMANN DIAGNOSTICS
1 Suprema Drive
Newport Coast, CA 92657
www.kilmanndiagnostics.com
info@kilmanndiagnostics.com
949.497.8766

ORGANIZATIONAL INFLUENCE SURVEY

Response Scale

Carefully study the response scale below. You will be asked to use the five numbers on this scale to record your responses to the 60 items in this survey. To ensure an accurate assessment, please keep these categories clearly in mind while you respond to the survey. You may refer back to this page at any time.

1   I need to have *much less influence* than I now have. Others are in a better position to make the decision or shape the outcome.

2   I need to have *less influence* on this aspect of my organization than I now have. My performance and satisfaction would increase if others played more of a role in making the decision or shaping the outcome.

3   I have as much influence on this aspect as I need. If the current balance of influence between me and the organization shifted, my performance and satisfaction would decrease.

4   I need to have *more influence* on this aspect of my organization than I now have. My performance and satisfaction would increase if others played less of a role in making the decision or shaping the outcome.

5   I need to have *much more influence* than I now have. I am in the best position to make the decision or shape the outcome.

ORGANIZATIONAL INFLUENCE SURVEY

Instructions

For each item listed below, please circle the number that indicates the extent to which you need to have less or more influence than you now have **to improve your job performance and satisfaction**. While some of these items concern just your own work group or your coworkers, other items consider *other* work groups, departments, or the organization as a whole. Even if these latter work units seem somewhat removed from your daily activities, you should still respond according to what you need to influence in order to improve your performance and job satisfaction.

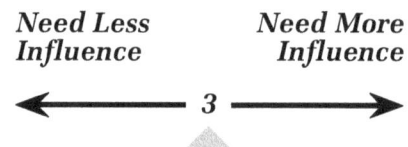

	Need Less Influence ←——— 3 ———→ *Need More Influence*				
1. My daily work schedule.	1	2	3	4	5
2. My organization's strategic goals.	1	2	3	4	5
3. The work habits of my coworkers.	1	2	3	4	5
4. The amount of cooperation between departments.	1	2	3	4	5
5. Who is assigned to work with me.	1	2	3	4	5

ORGANIZATIONAL INFLUENCE SURVEY

		Need Less Influence			Need More Influence	
		←		3 ▲		→
		1	2	3	4	5
6.	My organization's performance appraisal system.	1	2	3	4	5
7.	How my coworkers treat one another.	1	2	3	4	5
8.	How various interdepartmental conflicts are addressed.	1	2	3	4	5
9.	The objectives and tasks of my work group.	1	2	3	4	5
10.	How my organization is divided into areas and departments.	1	2	3	4	5
11.	The cooperation I receive from my own work group.	1	2	3	4	5
12.	The amount of recognition that people receive for doing well.	1	2	3	4	5
13.	The location of my office or work space.	1	2	3	4	5

ORGANIZATIONAL INFLUENCE SURVEY

		Need Less Influence			Need More Influence	
		←		3	→	
14.	The corporate fringe benefits program.	1	2	3	4	5
15.	The morale in my work group.	1	2	3	4	5
16.	Whether corporate decisions and actions are ethical.	1	2	3	4	5
17.	The resources that I need to do my job.	1	2	3	4	5
18.	The quality of my organization's products and services.	1	2	3	4	5
19.	Whether my coworkers take risks.	1	2	3	4	5
20.	The image of my area or department.	1	2	3	4	5
21.	The training that I receive to improve my skills.	1	2	3	4	5

		Need Less Influence			Need More Influence	
		←		3	→	
22.	The base salary I receive for my training and experience.	1	2	3	4	5
23.	Whether my boss listens to my ideas.	1	2	3	4	5
24.	The grapevine and gossip throughout my organization.	1	2	3	4	5
25.	Hiring decisions in my work group.	1	2	3	4	5
26.	The clarity of organizational goals and objectives.	1	2	3	4	5
27.	The amount of pressure that is put on me to perform well.	1	2	3	4	5
28.	How interdepartmental meetings are conducted.	1	2	3	4	5
29.	When I arrive at work and when I leave.	1	2	3	4	5

ORGANIZATIONAL INFLUENCE SURVEY

	Need Less Influence		Need More Influence	

← 3 →

		1	2	3	4	5
30.	The overall success of my organization.	1	2	3	4	5
31.	How my coworkers perceive me.	1	2	3	4	5
32.	The information provided about other areas and departments.	1	2	3	4	5
33.	How the performance review system is conducted in my group.	1	2	3	4	5
34.	The allocation of resources to areas and departments.	1	2	3	4	5
35.	Whether my work group brings differences out into the open.	1	2	3	4	5
36.	The general team spirit in my organization.	1	2	3	4	5
37.	How hard my coworkers try to do a good job.	1	2	3	4	5

ORGANIZATIONAL INFLUENCE SURVEY

		Need Less Influence			Need More Influence	
		⟵		3	⟶	
38.	Major capital investments in plants and equipment.	1	2	3	4	5
39.	The decisions made in work group meetings.	1	2	3	4	5
40.	The reputation of my organization.	1	2	3	4	5
41.	How my job priorities are adjusted from day to day.	1	2	3	4	5
42.	Corporate rules and regulations.	1	2	3	4	5
43.	How others plan and organize my work for the day.	1	2	3	4	5
44.	Whether departments treat one another with respect.	1	2	3	4	5
45.	The number of work group meetings I am required to attend.	1	2	3	4	5

ORGANIZATIONAL INFLUENCE SURVEY

		Need Less Influence ←—— 3 ——→ *Need More Influence*				
46.	The corporate system of job classification and salary grades.	*1*	*2*	*3*	*4*	*5*
47.	Whether my coworkers trust one another.	*1*	*2*	*3*	*4*	*5*
48.	The morale in other departments in the organization.	*1*	*2*	*3*	*4*	*5*
49.	When I can schedule my vacation.	*1*	*2*	*3*	*4*	*5*
50.	The number of management levels in my organization.	*1*	*2*	*3*	*4*	*5*
51.	How I spend my lunch break.	*1*	*2*	*3*	*4*	*5*
52.	Whether top management is given honest feedback.	*1*	*2*	*3*	*4*	*5*
53.	Promotion decisions in my own department.	*1*	*2*	*3*	*4*	*5*

ORGANIZATIONAL INFLUENCE SURVEY

		Need Less Influence			Need More Influence	
		←		3		→
54.	Key promotions in other areas or departments.	1	2	3	4	5
55.	How my work group feels about itself.	1	2	3	4	5
56.	Corporate reactions to risk taking and doing things in new ways.	1	2	3	4	5
57.	Being assigned to work on special projects or committees.	1	2	3	4	5
58.	The annual performance of my organization.	1	2	3	4	5
59.	How my coworkers approach their job-related problems.	1	2	3	4	5
60.	The amount of socializing that occurs across departmental lines.	1	2	3	4	5

Scoring Your Responses

In the spaces next to the items on the following page, please transfer the numbers you circled on the previous pages of this survey. You will find it easiest to transfer your responses—in order—from item 1 through 60. Be sure that you accurately transfer every number.

Next, please add up each of the four columns. The resulting sums are your scores for four *influence domains:* Formal-Inside, Formal-Outside, Informal-Inside, and Informal-Outside. The meaning and implications of these four influence domains will be discussed shortly.

ORGANIZATIONAL INFLUENCE SURVEY

1. ___   2. ___   3. ___   4. ___

5. ___   6. ___   7. ___   8. ___

9. ___   10. ___   11. ___   12. ___

13. ___   14. ___   15. ___   16. ___

17. ___   18. ___   19. ___   20. ___

21. ___   22. ___   23. ___   24. ___

25. ___   26. ___   27. ___   28. ___

29. ___   30. ___   31. ___   32. ___

33. ___   34. ___   35. ___   36. ___

37. ___   38. ___   39. ___   40. ___

41. ___   42. ___   43. ___   44. ___

45. ___   46. ___   47. ___   48. ___

49. ___   50. ___   51. ___   52. ___

53. ___   54. ___   55. ___   56. ___

57. ___   58. ___   59. ___   60. ___

Sum: Formal-Inside	Sum: Formal-Outside	Sum: Informal-Inside	Sum: Informal-Outside

Graphing Your Scores

On the opposite page, record each of your four individual scores in the space provided next to its corresponding influence domain.

Each influence domain is subdivided into three connecting triangles, representing different ranges of all possible scores: The middle triangle in each domain covers the scores from 40 to 50 (the middle of the range). The triangle on the left covers the scores from 15 to 39 (the lower part of the range). The triangle on the right covers the scores from 51 to 75 (the higher part of the range).

For each influence domain, locate the specific triangle that includes your score. Then, use either a pen or pencil to shade that triangle only. For example, if your score for Formal-Inside is 25, you would shade just the triangle on the left (since this number falls between 15 and 39). If your score for Formal-Outside is 45, you would shade just the middle triangle (since this number falls between 40 and 50). If your score for Informal-Inside is 65, you would shade only the triangle on the right (since this number falls between 51 and 75), and so forth. Thus, for each influence domain, shade just one of the three available triangles:

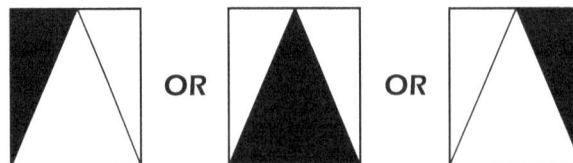

ORGANIZATIONAL INFLUENCE SURVEY

My Influence Scores

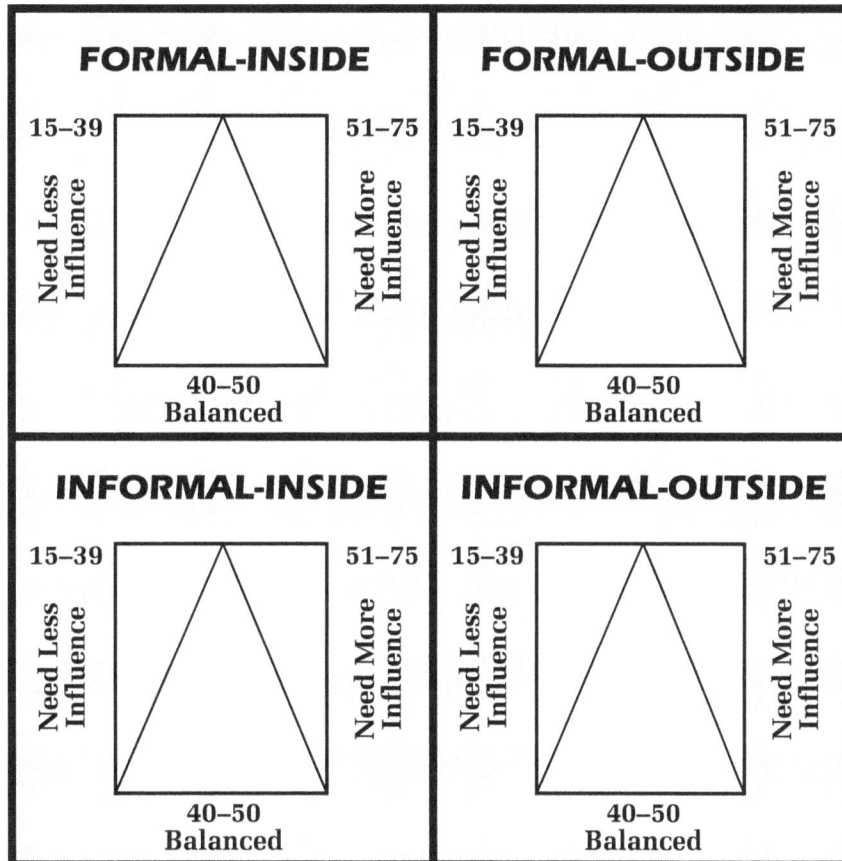

SCORE ___

SCORE ___

FORMAL-INSIDE

15–39
Need Less Influence

51–75
Need More Influence

40–50
Balanced

FORMAL-OUTSIDE

15–39
Need Less Influence

51–75
Need More Influence

40–50
Balanced

INFORMAL-INSIDE

15–39
Need Less Influence

51–75
Need More Influence

40–50
Balanced

INFORMAL-OUTSIDE

15–39
Need Less Influence

51–75
Need More Influence

40–50
Balanced

SCORE ___

SCORE ___

Developing Organizational Profiles

Once all the people in your work group have obtained and graphed their scores on the four influence domains, collect all these numbers together on a sheet of paper and then calculate four averages: a group average for Formal-Inside, Formal-Outside, Informal-Inside, and Informal-Outside. While computing these four averages, be sure to divide the sum of the scores in each domain by the right number of individuals in your group: those who actually provided their scores for these calculations.

Once the four averages have been calculated for your work group, please enter the results in the appropriate spaces on the opposite page. Then, as you did for your own influence scores, use a pen or pencil to shade the relevant triangles for **1. My Work Group.** Next, if you have access to the other work groups in your department, you can calculate and graph the four averages for **2. My Department.** And if you have access to all the departments in your organization, you can calculate and graph the four averages for **3. My Organization.** For your convenience, the next pages provide these additional profiles, including a space to enter the number of respondents (N) included in the analysis. *Note:* In calculating these various profiles, you might find it necessary to weight the averages of each work unit by the number of its members to adjust for different sizes of groups and departments in your organization.

1. My Work Group (N = _____)

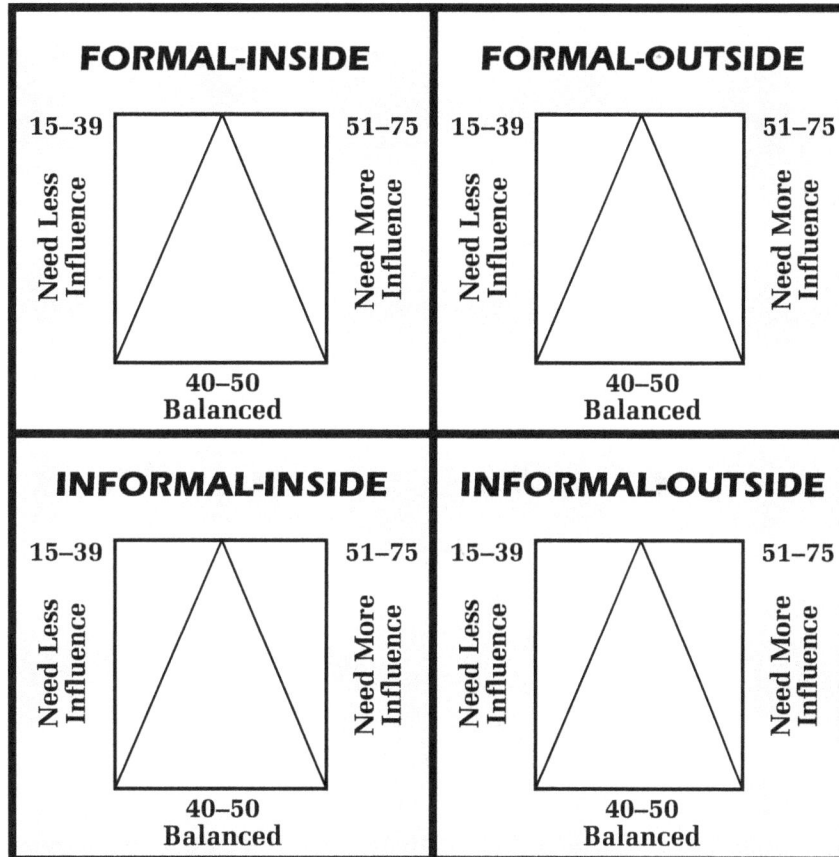

FORMAL-INSIDE

15–39   51–75

Need Less Influence   Need More Influence

40–50
Balanced

AVERAGE   _____ (left)
_____ AVERAGE (right)

FORMAL-OUTSIDE

15–39   51–75

Need Less Influence   Need More Influence

40–50
Balanced

INFORMAL-INSIDE

15–39   51–75

Need Less Influence   Need More Influence

40–50
Balanced

AVERAGE   _____ (left)
_____ AVERAGE (right)

INFORMAL-OUTSIDE

15–39   51–75

Need Less Influence   Need More Influence

40–50
Balanced

ORGANIZATIONAL INFLUENCE SURVEY

2. My Department (N = _____)

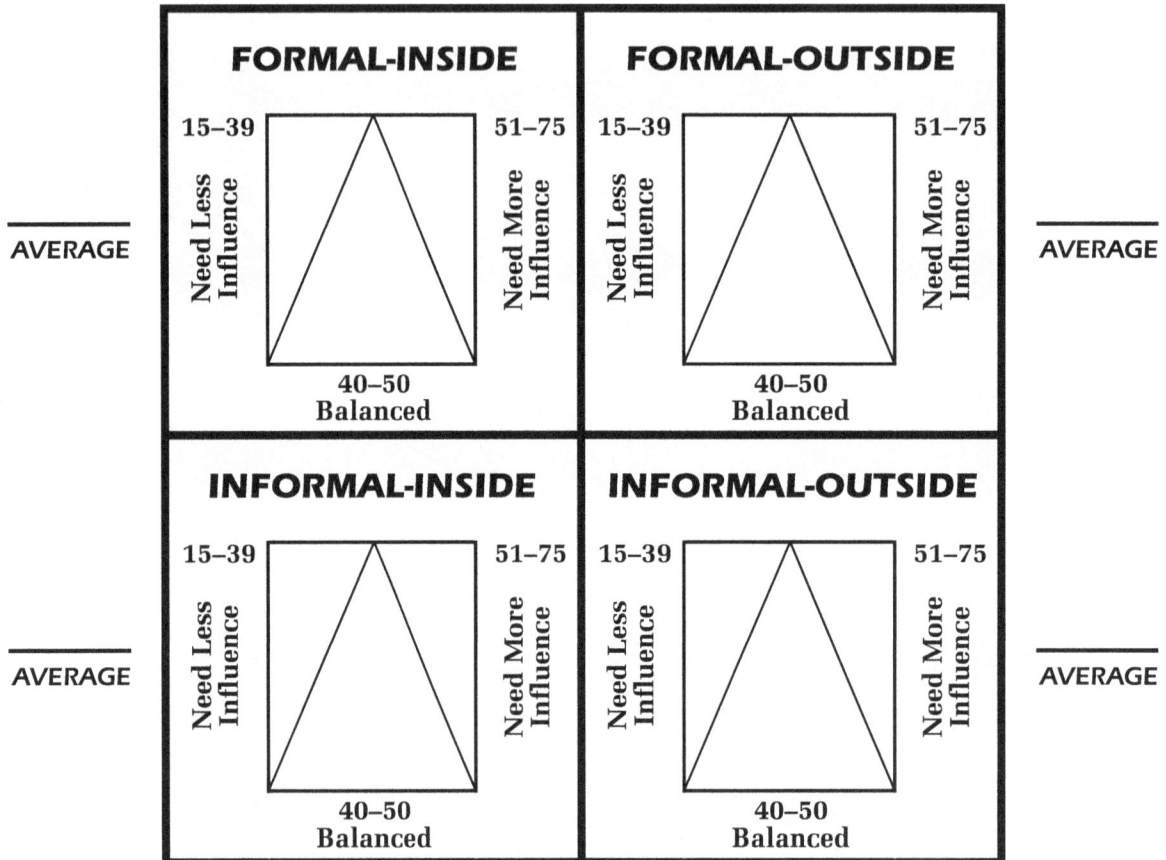

FORMAL-INSIDE

15–39   51–75

Need Less Influence   Need More Influence

40–50
Balanced

AVERAGE   _____

FORMAL-OUTSIDE

15–39   51–75

Need Less Influence   Need More Influence

40–50
Balanced

_____ AVERAGE

INFORMAL-INSIDE

15–39   51–75

Need Less Influence   Need More Influence

40–50
Balanced

AVERAGE   _____

INFORMAL-OUTSIDE

15–39   51–75

Need Less Influence   Need More Influence

40–50
Balanced

_____ AVERAGE

ORGANIZATIONAL INFLUENCE SURVEY

3. My Organization (N = _____)

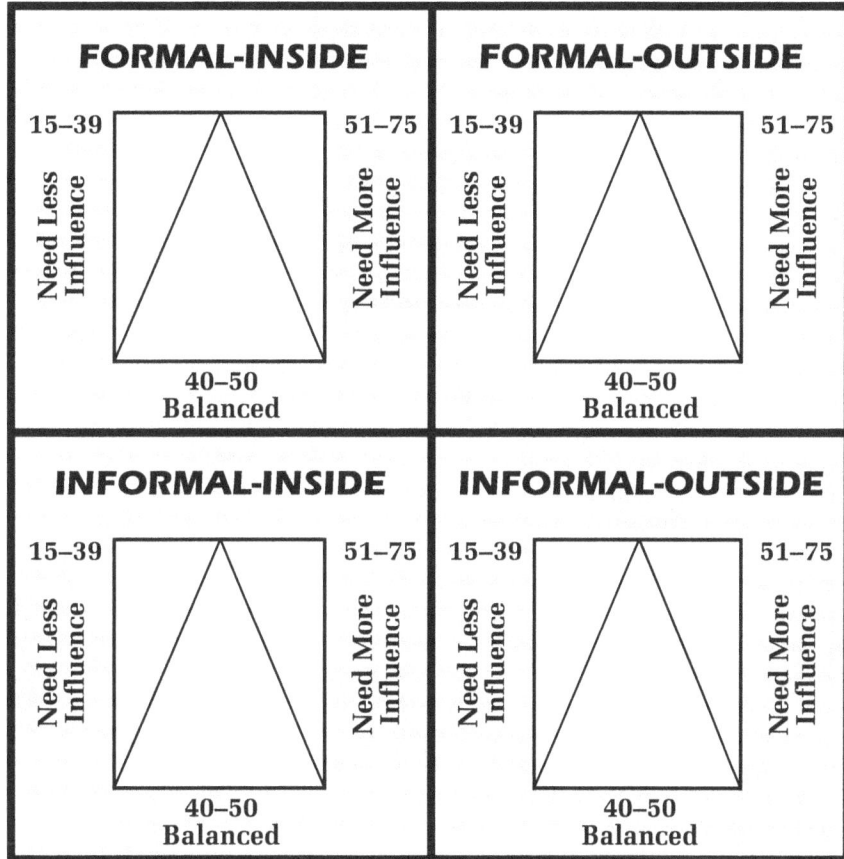

<table>
<tr><th colspan="2">FORMAL-INSIDE</th><th colspan="2">FORMAL-OUTSIDE</th></tr>
</table>

AVERAGE _____

FORMAL-INSIDE	
15–39	51–75
Need Less Influence	Need More Influence
40–50 Balanced	

AVERAGE _____

FORMAL-OUTSIDE	
15–39	51–75
Need Less Influence	Need More Influence
40–50 Balanced	

AVERAGE _____

INFORMAL-INSIDE	
15–39	51–75
Need Less Influence	Need More Influence
40–50 Balanced	

AVERAGE _____

INFORMAL-OUTSIDE	
15–39	51–75
Need Less Influence	Need More Influence
40–50 Balanced	

Defining Four Influence Domains

As shown below, the four influence domains are defined by two basic distinctions: (1) formal versus informal aspects of the organization that function (2) inside and outside your work group.

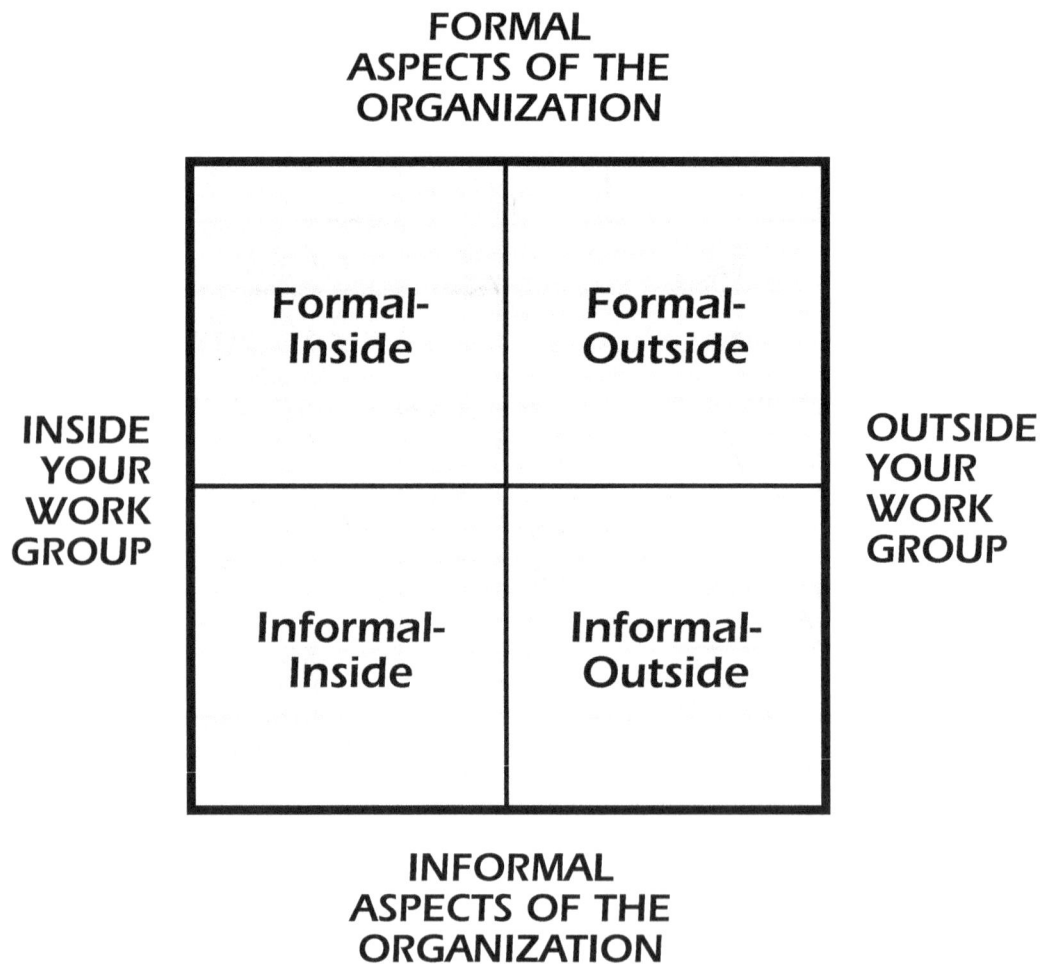

```
                    FORMAL
                 ASPECTS OF THE
                 ORGANIZATION

                 ┌──────────────┬──────────────┐
                 │              │              │
                 │   Formal-    │   Formal-    │
                 │   Inside     │   Outside    │
  INSIDE         │              │              │        OUTSIDE
  YOUR           ├──────────────┼──────────────┤        YOUR
  WORK           │              │              │        WORK
  GROUP          │  Informal-   │  Informal-   │        GROUP
                 │   Inside     │   Outside    │
                 │              │              │
                 └──────────────┴──────────────┘

                   INFORMAL
                 ASPECTS OF THE
                 ORGANIZATION
```

The first distinction recognizes two different kinds of "things" that can be influenced in an organization. The formal aspects include the whole variety of tangible—visible—resources: personnel, budgets, information, documents, buildings, technology, and equipment. The informal aspects include the full variety of human experiences in an organization: how people perceive, feel, think, and make decisions. These informal aspects also include how work groups and departments mirror—and sometimes magnify—interpersonal struggles. This most fundamental formal versus informal distinction ensures that both the "hard" and "soft" aspects of organizational life are included in any balance-of-influence analysis.

The second distinction specifies the location of the formal and informal aspects: inside the work group (including the boss) or outside the work group (including other work units and departments in the organization). This key distinction accepts that most people can influence what goes on inside their own group to a greater extent than what goes on in someone else's—let alone in other functional areas and hierarchical levels in their organization. Since decisions made by these others can greatly influence the performance and job satisfaction of any individual, however, it is important to include this "outside" perspective. Thus, the outside versus inside distinction ensures that all influence sources on an individual—however removed from the immediate work situation—are included in any balance-of-influence analysis.

The two key distinctions combine to yield the four influence domains:

Formal-Outside includes documents and systems that affect the whole organization: strategic goals, departmental structures, the allocation of resources, and the reward system.

Formal-Inside considers how these organization-wide documents and systems are formulated into detailed work-group objectives, priorities, budgets, schedules, and job assignments, as well as how the procedures for the reward system are determined and used inside the group.

Informal-Outside includes those organization-wide aspects that pertain to team spirit, cooperation, attitudes about risk taking, willingness to challenge ideas, information sharing, and mutual respect—beyond the jurisdiction of any group or department (for example, the organization's culture).

Informal-Inside includes how the work group manages the social and psychological aspects of its functioning by considering the amount of sharing, cooperation, mutual respect, and risk taking that occurs among coworkers in the same work group.

To inspect the specific items that are sorted into each influence domain, you can refer back to the four columns on the scoring sheet (see page 11) where the items composing each influence domain are listed.

Interpreting Your Scores

The best outcome that can be obtained from this survey is an acceptable **balance of influence** between individuals and their organization, which facilitates all efforts at improving performance and satisfaction. Such an outcome is illustrated in the profile shown below, where only the **middle triangles** are shaded in all four domains.

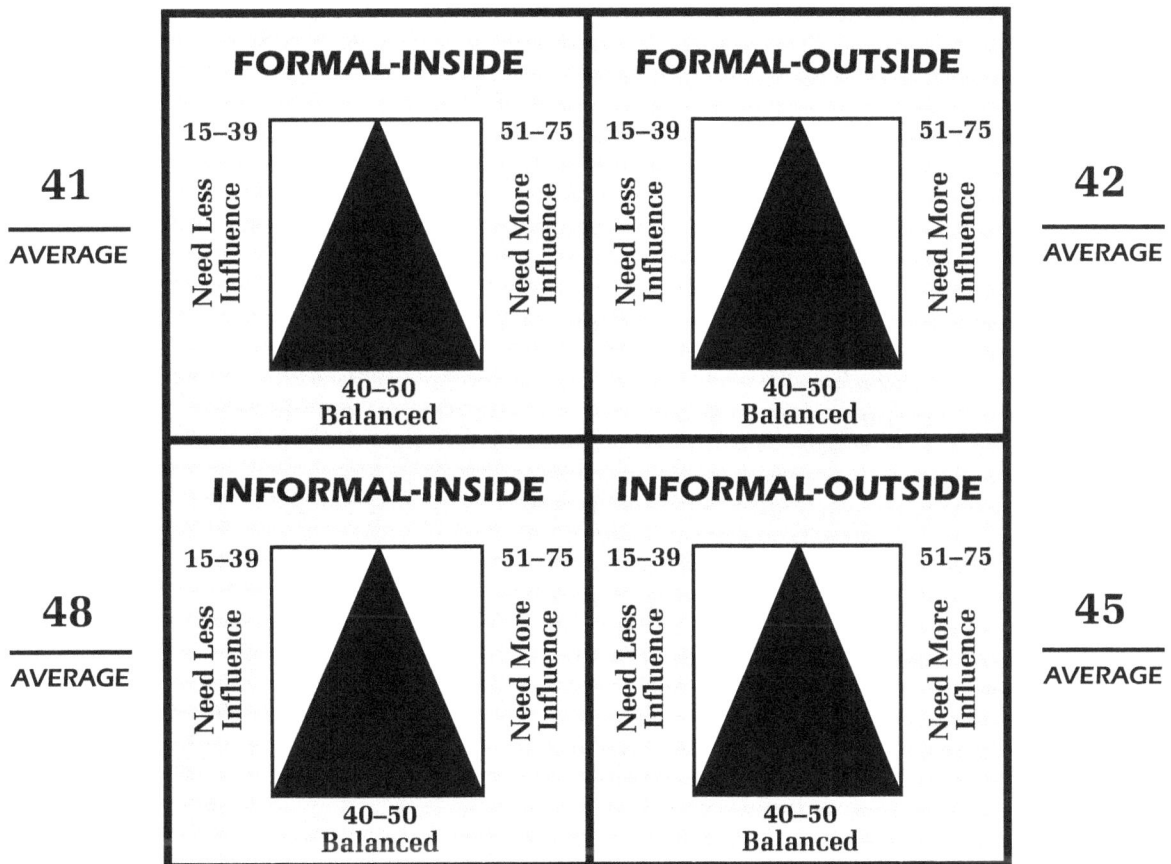

	FORMAL-INSIDE	FORMAL-OUTSIDE	
41 AVERAGE	15–39 / Need Less Influence ▲ 51–75 / Need More Influence / 40–50 Balanced	15–39 / Need Less Influence ▲ 51–75 / Need More Influence / 40–50 Balanced	**42** AVERAGE
48 AVERAGE	INFORMAL-INSIDE / 15–39 / Need Less Influence ▲ 51–75 / Need More Influence / 40–50 Balanced	INFORMAL-OUTSIDE / 15–39 / Need Less Influence ▲ 51–75 / Need More Influence / 40–50 Balanced	**45** AVERAGE

Most often, however, the "best" profile is not attained. Usually, at least one of the four influence domains deviates significantly from the mid range of the scale (40–50), which suggests that the balance of influence between individuals and their organizations is in need of adjustment. Moreover, when more than one domain of influence falls in either the left or right-side triangles, the imbalance of organizational influence is multidimensional, and, therefore, more complex. An imbalance in the formal aspects of the organization outside an individual's work group (for example, not having any say in determining what schedule changes are made for the whole department) may be aggravated inside the group by the careless way in which work is assigned on a daily basis (Formal-Inside). Or not only are the Informal-Outside aspects interfering with the quality of the work (for example, not getting the necessary cooperation from other departments), but the coworkers within the same group may mistrust one another (Informal-Inside) and, therefore, do not cooperate with one another either. In the extreme case in which *all four influence domains are imbalanced*, the prospects for creating and maintaining long-term organizational success are slim.

The following page shows a sample profile in which several domains deviate from a balance of influence, which pinpoints the directions for change and improvement: More influence is needed in Informal-Inside and Informal-Outside (perhaps due to a dysfunctional culture throughout the organization), although less influence is desired in Formal-Outside (perhaps due to unnecessary involvement in corporate matters that should be handled—not delegated—by senior executives).

ORGANIZATIONAL INFLUENCE SURVEY

An Example: Imbalance in Organizational Influence

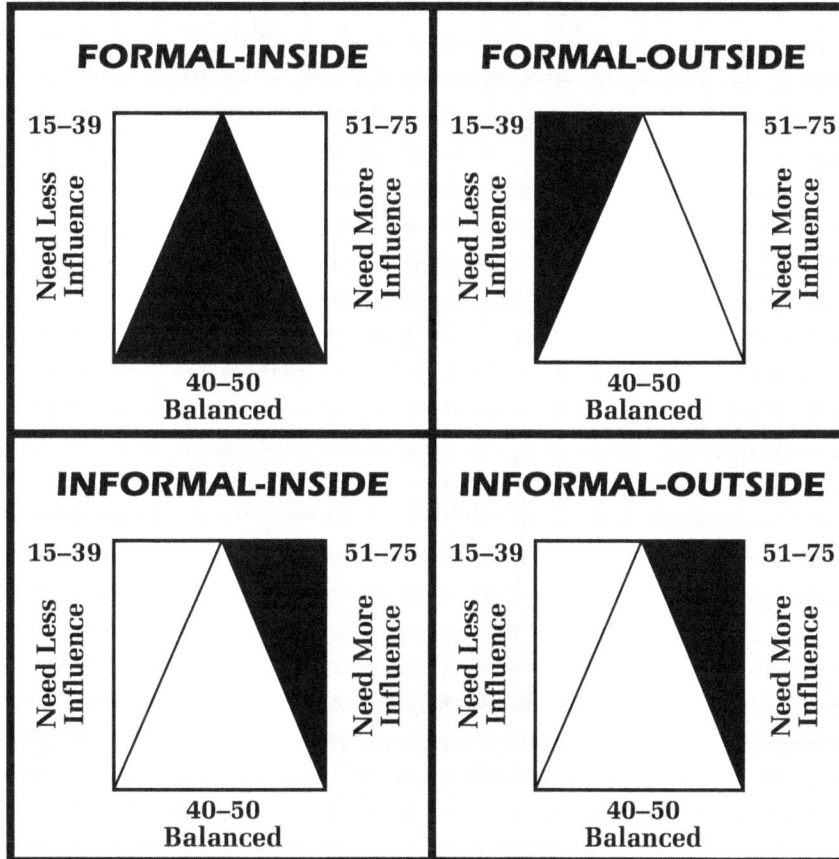

49 / AVERAGE	**FORMAL-INSIDE** — 15–39 Need Less Influence / 51–75 Need More Influence / 40–50 Balanced	**FORMAL-OUTSIDE** — 15–39 Need Less Influence / 51–75 Need More Influence / 40–50 Balanced	**27** / AVERAGE

49

AVERAGE

27

AVERAGE

FORMAL-INSIDE

15–39 Need Less Influence

51–75 Need More Influence

40–50 Balanced

FORMAL-OUTSIDE

15–39 Need Less Influence

51–75 Need More Influence

40–50 Balanced

67

AVERAGE

59

AVERAGE

INFORMAL-INSIDE

15–39 Need Less Influence

51–75 Need More Influence

40–50 Balanced

INFORMAL-OUTSIDE

15–39 Need Less Influence

51–75 Need More Influence

40–50 Balanced

Correcting Organizational Imbalances

A complete program for planned change has been designed to improve the formal and informal aspects of the organization—both inside and outside all work groups. The informal aspects are addressed by the first three tracks: (1) the culture track, (2) the skills track, and (3) the team track. The formal aspects of the organization are handled by the next two tracks: (4) the strategy-structure track and (5) the reward system track.

These tracks, in most cases, are scheduled in the prescribed order. The first three tracks improve the manner in which people (and work units) behave toward one another on the job. The next two tracks modify the organization's formal aspects—its documents, technologies, systems, and resources that guide what people in the organization are supposed to do. Without first improving the informal organization—inside and outside all work groups—adjustments to the formal systems would be cosmetic and, therefore, ineffective.

What does each track do for the organization? The culture track first enhances trust, communication, information sharing, and a willingness to change among coworkers—the conditions that must exist before any other improvement effort can succeed. Then the skills track provides all personnel with new ways of coping with people, problems, time, and conflict. Then the team track infuses the new culture and updated skills within and across all work units—thereby fostering cooperation through out the organization so that complex problems can be addressed with all the expertise and information available.

Regarding the formal systems of the organization, the strategy-structure track develops either a completely new or a revised strategic plan and then aligns departments, work groups, jobs, and all other resources with the new strategic direction. Lastly, the reward system track establishes a performance-based reward system—one that sustains all improvements by officially sanctioning the new culture, the use of updated skills, and cooperative team efforts within and across all work groups.

The figure below summarizes the important relationship between the four influence domains (the problem) and the five tracks (the solution):

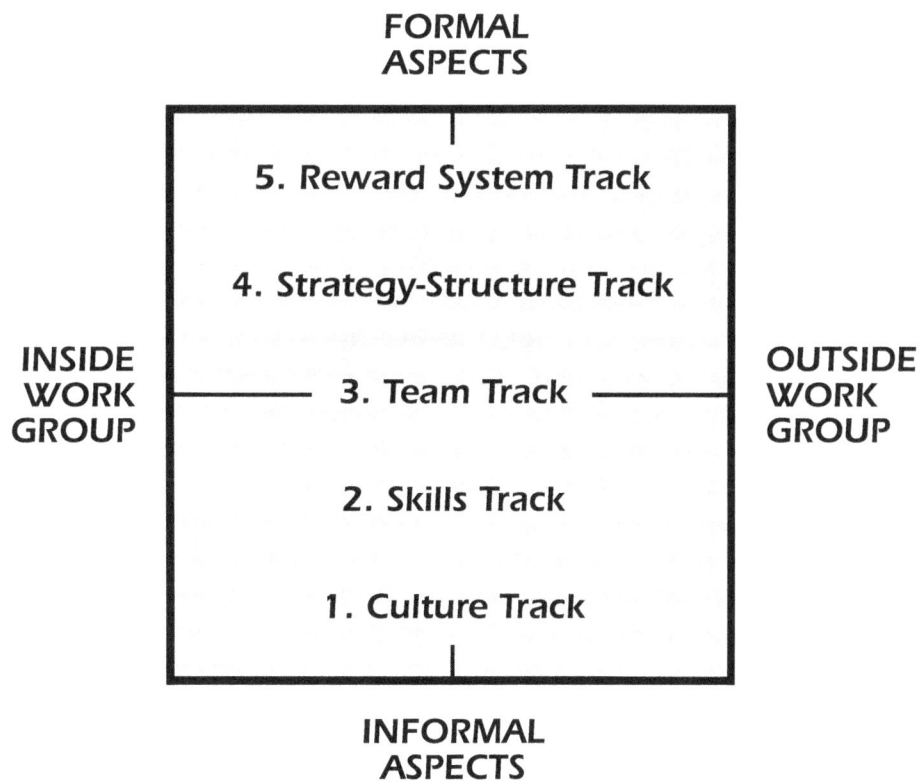

FORMAL
ASPECTS

5. Reward System Track

4. Strategy-Structure Track

INSIDE
WORK
GROUP —— 3. Team Track —— OUTSIDE
WORK
GROUP

2. Skills Track

1. Culture Track

INFORMAL
ASPECTS

The Challenge

Organizational influence is a two-way exchange: Organizations cannot accomplish their goals if they cannot influence their members to do the right things. And the members, of course, cannot do the right things— and satisfy their needs in the process—if they can't influence what goes on in their organizations.

On the one hand, those who occupy senior management positions in an organization usually influence much of what goes on—maybe too much. On the other hand, those who occupy nonsupervisory positions may not influence much at all—particularly outside their immediate work area. Rather than guessing whether you and your organization have the most effective balance of influence or not, this survey has enabled you to see which aspects of your organization you need to influence—less or more than you do now. Subsequently, your organization can improve both job performance and satisfaction by actively shifting the balance of influence with an integrated program of planned change. For further discussion of the theories and methods behind the five tracks, the interested reader is referred to R. H. Kilmann, *Beyond the Quick Fix* (Washington DC: Beard, 2004) as well as *Quantum Organizations* (Newport Coast, CA: Kilmann Diagnostics, 2011).

Assessment Tools for the Eight Tracks
Distributed by Kilmann Diagnostics

Kilmann-Saxton Culture-Gap® Survey

Kilmanns Organizational Belief Survey

Kilmanns Time-Gap Survey

Kilmanns Team-Gap Survey

Organizational Courage Assessment

Kilmann-Covin Organizational Influence Survey

Plus the Online Version of the
Thomas-Kilmann Conflict Mode Instrument

Plus These Training and Development Tools
Work Sheets for Identifying and Closing Culture-Gaps
Work Sheets for Identifying and Closing Team-Gaps

And the Book That Fully Explains the Eight Tracks
Quantum Organizations

www.ingramcontent.com/pod-product-compliance
Lightning Source LLC
Chambersburg PA
CBHW081205270326
41930CB00014B/3310